HOW TO SELL
YOUR HOUSE FOR
MORE MONEY
Now! Easy As 123soldnow.com

Kathy James

Kathy is a real estate investor, a licensed Realtor, business owner and successful author. She has been investing in real estate, buying and selling with clients and is active in property management since the 1980's. Kathy studied Industrial Design and Architecture at California State University Northridge. Her love of design, business and real estate make her the perfect asset to your real estate investments and related transactions. Whether you're buying or selling real estate, you will have the insider scoop for all of your business transactions from a genuine professional. Click on www.123soldnow.com

Disclaimer

The information in this book is provided as is. No part of this book is to be considered legal or financial advice. Discuss all such matters with your attorney and tax professional.

In memory of my Aunt Brigitte,

Who always encouraged and inspired me

To go beyond what I thought was possible

I will miss your guidance and love

You will always be remembered and live

Forever in our hearts.
2016

This Home has been my inspiration since I was nine years old.

It was definitely Love at first sight.

Fallingwater was built between 1936 and 1939 by Frank Lloyd Wright, America's most famous architect.

"The thing always happens that you really believe in; and the belief in a thing makes it happen."
— **Frank Lloyd Wright**

Contents

Chapter 1

Comparative market analysis
First things first, what's it worth
There's no substitute for experience, hire an expert

Chapter 2

Tricks of the trade
Curb appeal
Interior
Kitchen and Bathrooms
Take the home out of your house

Chapter 3

Staging the Bedrooms
Staging your Dining Room
Staging Closets
Stage the Outdoors

Chapter 4

The HOME Inspection
Getting ready
How much should you spend before selling

http://123soldnow.com

Chapter 5

Wash your windows
Conceal the critters
Light it up
Appeal to the senses
Always be ready to show

Chapter 6

Pricing it right

Chapter 7

What is a real estate investor
Sell quickly for less
Keep foreclosure off your credit rating
How an investor works
Sell Your Home Quickly

Chapter 8

Renting
Vacation Rentals

Chapter 9

I am here to help

http://123soldnow.com

How to sell your house for more money now!

Hi, I'm Kathy James. I am obsessed with houses. When I was nine years old living in Pittsburg Pennsylvania, out for an afternoon adventure with my parents, I remember walking through the woods. Then all of the sudden, out of nowhere, there was this most amazing house. I remember being stunned by my first vision of this home. It seemed to be growing out of the earth with the forest all around. Houses and architecture have been an obsession for me ever since. Can you guess which house I found in the middle of the woods? It was Fallingwater built by Frank Lloyd Wright, and there it was in the middle of the woods and it fascinated me. In the years that followed I went to any open house I came across. I studied design and architecture in college, and started collecting houses.

I may not know you personally but I do know you're looking to sell your home because you are reading this book. I am going to share some real estate secrets with you. Whether you're selling your property because of a job change; growing family, financial troubles or you owe more than your property is worth or anything in between. You will get the information and guidance you need to know in the pages that follow. As a seller, your primary objective is to sell your home quickly and for the most money possible. I will show you how to do just that. In this book, I will share with you the insider secrets to selling your house for more then what you thought you could and faster than you thought possible; secrets other realtors don't want you to know follow in the pages below.

Http://123soldnow.com

http://123soldnow.com

Sell it for more or sell it now

Selling a home can be an emotionally and physically exhausting process. I will explain two options for selling your home, one requires very little time and effort. The other includes some basic sprucing up to help get top dollar for your home. The information provided here will help you as a homeowner, identify which selling option is right you. Selling your home the traditional way or sell your home for quick cash now. I will provide you with tips for the selling journey ahead.

I have been in the real estate business for over twenty-five years and I know what it takes to get your home sold for more money and in less time, regardless of the reason why you have chosen to sell. I have worked with home owners who owed more than their house is worth or are behind in payments. Similarly I have also worked with sellers who have decided it's just time for more space or it is time to downsize. I have also worked with investors and first time home buyers. I am going to share some of the insider secrets I have learned over the years as an investor and as an agent with you in this book.

Houses are my obsession, I have bought and sold more homes than I can count and have worked with countless investors, real estate agents and first time home buyers. Additionally, I have managed more income property then the average person will in a lifetime.

My journey into real estate started way back in 1981 when my parents purchased a home forty-five-minutes north of where we were living in Santa Monica, California. At the time, I was eighteen-years-old and I did not want to move into their new home with them. Like any other eighteen-year-old, I wanted to stay in my home and stay with my friends while I went to college in my home town.

The apartment I shared with my parents in Santa Monica was just six blocks from the ocean, three bedrooms and two baths. Being the determined adolescent I was, I realized I needed to get some roommates to stay in the apartment. Rent amounted to 600 dollars per month and my two roommates each paid to rent one of the bedrooms in the apartment from me, thus started my journey of positive cash flow from rental income. Each month my roommates both paid enough money to cover the rent and I was able to live in my apartment rent free while attending Santa Monica College. What's not to love, right? I was instantly hooked on rental income.

After about two years I was able to obtain the apartment directly next door to mine and before you could turn around I had another three roommates, a total of five. By this point in my life I was not only living rent free but had positive cash flow each month from having five rooms rented. Fortunately, I was able to save the positive income and purchased my first investment property when I was 26 years old.

Initially I had searched in Santa Monica, Venice and other areas surrounding Los Angeles for my new investment property, however prices were high and I had developed an undeniable love for Phoenix, Arizona. Over the years I had visited the valley often and would look at the real estate section of the Sunday paper weekly. Often comparing the listings to those in Los Angeles, I was always amazed by the affordability and I ended up buying a four bedroom house in Phoenix.

Prior to my purchase, during the house hunting experience, I wanted everything in a house and had little money. It took some time, but I managed to find the perfect house at the right price. In addition to the income from my roommates covering the down payment, I was even able to cover the monthly mortgage with the income from the renters.

During my first nine months of home ownership, I was between Phoenix and Santa Monica spending a week in each city before I decided to move into the four bedroom home in Phoenix full time. My initial goal was to rent it out and make more positive cash flow but as fate would have it, my first child was on the way and I felt it would be a better quality of life to live in the investment property I purchased in Phoenix. Knowing that positive cash flow was a good thing and having roommates, or renters, was easy for me to handle, I went on the hunt for more income producing real estate.

http://123soldnow.com

Shortly after moving to Phoenix, I purchased a duplex. The duplex payment was about $450 per-month and I was able to rent one of the units for $450 covering the cost and gaining more positive cash flow each month from the second unit in the duplex. By now, I was still collecting rent from five roommates in Santa Monica and the two units in the duplex in Phoenix.

Another two years later, my second child was on the way and I knew I needed to let go of the apartments in Santa Monica as managing the renters became difficult while living a state away with an infant. I was faced with a big question: how do I replace the income from the five roommates? Hooked on real estate and religiously reading the real estate section in the Sunday paper every week, I came across an apartment complex and knew I had to have it. The complex had thirty-five units, made up by nine buildings with the property taking up an entire city block. Negotiations took place resulting in my ownership of the property, and after some reorganizing, cleaning, fixing, remodeling, I was able to get all thirty-five apartments rented and enjoyed positive cash flow each month.

In the years that followed I continued to purchase at least one single family property every year, sold the apartment complex and purchased two condos on a beach in Mexico which I turned into vacation rentals.

Over the course of this time, I met so many real estate agents, many of which I did not like for the simple fact that most of the agents I worked with had no idea of what was, or was not, a good investment property. In fact, most of the agents I worked with during this time did not own property themselves which still amazes me today.

The agents I worked with had no property management experience and did not understand what an investor was looking for. Typically they would show me three homes and expect I purchase one of the three they showed me. I have learned that while there are many stellar real estate agents that do go above and beyond the call of duty and know how to get the job done, you will not find many real estate agents that are real estate investors, have worked with investors, or have years of experience as a landlord as well as being an agent for buyers and sellers. Frustrated with my options, I decided the only way to get what I wanted was to become an agent myself.

While being an agent, I have worked with fix-and-flip properties, helped first time home buyers purchase a property, and have proved to be an incredible asset to an investor looking for their next property.

Chronicled in this book are my years of experience of being a real estate investor, a landlord, and real estate agent helping buyers and sellers of all kinds accomplish their goals. Because of all of all my experience in the industry I know what it takes to help home owners sell their homes for more money and in record time. I know houses.

Purchasing a home is an exhilarating and can be a confusing experience. On the other hand selling your largest asset can be very emotional and scary. It is such a rewarding experience for me to be able to help and guide you through the process. I am truly blessed to be able to give back in this way and share my years of experience and knowledge with you.

I look forward to assisting you in getting the most out of your property, whatever your circumstance may be; please always feel free to reach out to me.

Together we are going to:

> ➢ Check out your local market
> ➢ Get a Comparative Market Analysis (CMA) on your home
> ➢ Decide to sell your home retail and get it ready to sell
> ➢ Dress up, market, and otherwise set your house apart from the rest
> ➢ Decide which repairs need to be made and which repairs do not
> ➢ Decide on the right price
> ➢ Consider selling your home to an investor for a super-fast sale
> ➢ Hire the best professionals to help you along the way
> ➢ Look at rental options
> ➢ Negotiate and successfully close the sale.

Chapter 1

You can get your FREE CMA by going to:

http://123soldnow.com/

whatsmyhomeworth

Make Sure You Can Afford to Sell and get a CMA for your property

It only makes sense to sell your home if your proceeds are going to put cash in your pocket, though unfortunately, many people who bought a home in the peak bubble years of 2007 and 2008 are still not in a position to sell. If you fall into this category, there are still some options to consider. For example, you may be able to rent your home or if you really need to move, consider a short sale. In either case, I will help you figure out how much money you'll walk away with when it's all said and done.

The first step in this process is to figure out how much your home is worth and how much you will make from selling your home. This is where the Comparative Market Analysis (CMA) comes in. Keep in mind when determining what you will walk away with after the sale isn't as easy as subtracting your outstanding mortgage from the price you hope to get. You will have to pay a number of fees when you sell your home, such as the buyer agent commission, taxes, title insurance and other closing costs, which can vary by region and transaction.

What is a comparative market analysis?

A comparative market analysis (CMA) is an evaluation of similar, recently sold homes, also known as comparables. Comparables are homes of similar size, condition, age, and style that recently sold in a certain neighborhood.

The Comparative Market Analysis tool is often used to help determine the fair market value for a home. CMA establishes the current market value of the home and is prepared by a real estate agent. However, a CMA is not the same as an appraisal which is performed by a licensed appraiser.

First things first, what's it worth?

The CMA will provide you with information about houses similar to yours in size, amenities, and location, which are either on the market, have sold, or were listed but expired within a reasonably recent time period. It's ideal to have your CMA look back no more than three months when the market is in transition and no more than six months in a more stable market.

A good CMA can tell you:

➢ What homes like yours are actually selling for today
➢ How long it's taking them to sell
➢ What their sale prices were in relation to their list prices (the difference between what people actually got for their house and what the list price was).

When looking at your CMA, it's especially important to pay attention to the prices of pending homes, as well as recent closed sales, because they are the most recent transactions and will give you the best overview of what is selling and for how much in your neighborhood.

I also recommend you take the opportunity, either on your own or with your real estate agent, to visit some of the comparables yourself, and see if

http://123soldnow.com

they live up to the CMA estimate in terms of price, size, location, fixtures and other features. In other words, let's check out the competition! Put yourself in the mindset of the buyer, see what else is on the market and identify what makes your home different from the rest of the competition.

> **Get your FREE CMA today, just go to**
> http://123soldnow.com/whatsmyhomeworth

There's no substitute for experience, hire an expert

You might be wondering why you need a realtor to sell and market your property when you can easily post on Craigslist, Facebook, and on other social media. You will want a proactive plan for exposing your home to as many buyers as possible and ensure your home gives a great first impression. Social media and listing websites are great and while realtors utilize them, they also have access to thousands of potential buyers through other tools that are not accessible to the non-licensed real estate professional.

Realtors have access to post your home on the Multiple Listing Service, more commonly referred to as the MLS, in addition to posting your home on any of the hundreds of websites accessed through the MLS, including Zillow, Trulia, Realtor.com to name a few.

All of the marketing is time consuming and costly. On average, the realtor will spend around one percent of the sales price on marketing alone to make your home stand out.

Other highlights to selling your home with a realtor:

- ➢ Advise you on home repairs or updates
- ➢ Advise you on sales price for your home based on the latest market data
- ➢ Actively marketing your home to buyers
- ➢ Scheduling showings with potential buyers

http://123soldnow.com

- ➢ Negotiating to get the best price on your home
- ➢ Handling all the required paperwork

A common reason some sellers choose not to use a realtor is because they believe they know how much they want for it and don't want a relator telling them how much they should sell it for. It is not the realtor's job to determine the selling price of your home. However it is the realtor's job to advise you and educate you on the current market by providing comparable property prices in addition to giving you a realistic idea of what your home can sell for as well as its potential appraised value. It is important to keep in mind that the sales price and appraised value are not always the same.

Another common concern is that all the realtor cares about is commission and won't necessarily keep the sellers best interests in mind. Keep in mind that the realtor is working for you. It is best to meet with potential realtors before ever agreeing to list your home, because just like everything in life, not all realtors are created equal. It is important to find a realtor who will sit down and listen to your wants, needs, and will answer your questions to make your home selling experience stress free. A common term for meeting with a perspective agent is called a listing appointment.

Selling your property without a licensed real estate agent guarantees one thing: You will make mistakes. Some of these mistakes could be small, while others could drastically affect the sales price of the house. For sale by owner, or FSBO sellers, struggle most with the paperwork associated with selling their home as well as pricing and preparing their home for the sale. A real estate agent will advise you based on experience, not emotion.

Would you rather save $6,250 or make $27,000? According to Dave Ramsey, a New York Times bestselling author and America's trusted voice on Money, "your home is a big investment, and you want to make the most of it."

For the typical "For Sale by Owner" (FSBO) in 2014 the average price of home sold was $208,000. According to the National Association of Realtors

(NAR), the typical home sold by an agent in 2014 fetched $235,000. That's a $27,000 difference.

"Keeping the agent commission all to yourself seems like an easy way to get more out of the sale of your home," said Ramsey, adding "the problem is you're leaving even more money on the table by opting out of using a pro."

Ramsey also noted that selling your home on your own doesn't necessarily mean an agent-free transaction. "You still owe it to the buyer's agent to pay their commission. After all, they worked hard to get their buyer into your home. If they get 3% of the sale, you can cut your $12,500 in savings in half, leaving you $6,250."

There are always exceptions and you might be able to pull off a FSBO sale if you have bought and sold half a dozen homes of your own or you live in a sought-after neighborhood where homes sell in two days. If you aren't the exception to these circumstances, like the 88 percent of  buyers who used a real estate agent to buy their homes according to a recent NAR report, then let a professional guide you through the process.

Real estate contracts are extremely complicated and there are so many disclosure laws now that a seller needs to be aware of that you will need a professional to help you understand the contract and the process. Forgoing an expert means you are accepting liability.

A realtor knows what's selling around you and for what price. When an offer comes in, they can tell you whether it is reasonable and help you negotiate smartly. Sometimes what may seem like a big problem to the seller may be something the real estate agent has encountered many times before. Because of this, realtors typically have connections with handymen, contractors, carpet layers, granite installers, gardeners, pool servicers, and everything else you could possibly need.

Chapter 2

Option One

The traditional sale: Sell your home with basic upgrades to get top dollar

We are going to cover the first of the two options for selling your home: the traditional sale. This option includes some basic sprucing up and upgrades to get the top dollar for your home.

Tricks of the trade to help you get top dollar when selling your home

In this section we will look at simple things you, the seller, can do to improve your home and ensure top dollar when selling.

Numerous studies show that a house that is well polished on the surface and staged properly will appeal to more buyers, sell faster, and most importantly, sell for more money. The goal is to make your home look good, but don't spend too much. In my experience, I have noticed that typically quick fixes before selling always pay off more as opposed to spending tons of money on huge makeovers.

Here are some of the findings from the 2015 Remodeling Cost Vs. Value report:

http://123soldnow.com

Projects that deliver the highest percentage of return on investment

➢ Entry door replacement (steel): 101.8%
➢ Garage door replacement: 88.4%
➢ Siding replacement (fiber-cement): 84.3%
➢ Siding replacement (vinyl): 80.7%
➢ Deck addition (wood): 80.5%

Renovation projects that deliver the lowest percentage of return on investment

➢ Sunroom addition: 48.5%
➢ Home office remodel: 48.7%
➢ Master suite addition: 53.7%
➢ Garage addition: 54.7%
➢ Bathroom addition: 57.8%

You may not be able to improve the market value of your house, but you can improve its marketability. Remember: first impressions count the most. Basically it boils down to this, in my experience home buyers are looking for the more move in ready home. The better it looks the faster it will sell.

Curb appeal

Being a real estate investor for years and as an agent with buyers, I have arrived at a property countless times, and just on curb appeal alone have decided not to get out of the car and go into the home. As superficial as it sounds, I'm not kidding. It happens more often than you would think. Buyers will immediately look for a well-kept yard, clean driveway, and take in the overall appearance of the house. If well kept, it will increase the likelihood that buyers will want to see more. When it comes to selling your home, it's now more important than ever to focus on ways to add value and design appeal to your home's exterior.

According to Niki Decker, real estate expert and creator of "National Curb Appeal Month," potential home buyers make a "street decision" in less than 12 seconds on whether or not to view a home that's for sale. It's easy to understand the importance of curb appeal and making a good first impression.

Go out into the street and take a look at your home. Really take a good look and look for potential shortcomings. Ask yourself, is it attractive, clean, and well-kept, or does it need maintenance that you have been putting off? Does the home look inviting, clean and well kept? Is it messy or dirty? What do you see? Remember, driving into the driveway and walking up to your front door sets the stage for your home and your buyers expectations.

After you've been in a home for a while, it can be difficult to see it objectively. So take suggestions from a real estate professional, friends, or family about how to make it look better and keep in mind that regardless of if you are a home buyer or seller, everyone wants a house that looks great from the curb.

Can your homes curb appeal be improved? You bet it can. This could mean adding new sod, planting flowers, painting the front door or replacing the mailbox. Sometimes trimming trees and bushes so buyers can actually see the house works wonders. Don't forget to clear the weeds and unsightly items from the front of the house.

This is also a good time to make a statement with your front door. Buyers will linger at the door while they wait for the agent to open the lockbox so consider options with decorative glass access and stunning sidelights to add more natural light while maintaining a sense of style and privacy.

Take a look at your home itself; you may need to pressure-wash the driveway, front walkway or the house and patio. Cleaning and painting the front of the home as well as the garage door, to make a good first impression is a good thing. After all you only get to give a first impression once.

No matter how good the interior of your home looks, buyers have already judged your home before they walk through the front door. If you put money into cleaning up the outside of your home I can guarantee that buyers will be more likely to take a tour of the inside of your home. Curb appeal is what draws buyers in, helps maintain their interest, and sets your home apart from the competition.

Interior

Entryways are the first area inside your home that a prospective home buyer will see. You use it as a utility space for your coat, shoes and keys but when you're selling, make it welcoming by putting in a small bench, a vase of fresh-cut flowers or even some cookies. In the event you only had enough time and money to invest in one area of the house, you should invest it in the area or room that is seen first upon entry through the front door.

Painting is one of the least expensive ways to freshen up your home for sale, and it can cost upwards of $300 a room if you're hiring a pro to do your entire home. You can save big by painting just a few select areas like high-traffic rooms, the kitchen and bathrooms and any rooms with brightly-painted walls. You can save even more by doing the project yourself – a gallon of paint averages about $30. If you can take a chip of paint off of your wall, have the paint matched at home depot or Lowes, you will be able to get the job done in a quick hurry, and not have to paint every square inch. I use the same color in all of my rental properties and when tenants move out, touch up is fast and easy. Again I cannot impress upon you enough what a difference fresh clean paint makes in a property.

One of the best ways to get your home ready to show to prospective buyers is to depersonalize it by removing family photos, quirky art and collectibles, and vibrant paint colors. Don't take it personally, but no one likes your pet accessories, over-stuffed closets, movie collections, and clutter, except you. Simplify and neutralize your home as if it were a model home, because guess what, that's exactly what it is going to be while it's on the market for sale. Your goal is to create a soothing space that allows buyers to visualize their own family and lifestyle in the home--not yours. Make sure your walls are clean, the space is decluttered, and that everything looks neat and tidy. This might be a really good time for you to start packing; after all you are planning to move.

Other easy updates include new fixtures and hardware. Be sure to pick something that looks clean and fresh, in addition to being on trend with what is in style. For ideas of what is in style get a few home magazines and also take a look at http://www.houzz.com.

Kitchen and Bathrooms

The benefits of remodeling your kitchen are endless and the best part of it is that you will probably get 85 percent of your money back. It may be a few thousand dollars to replace countertops where a buyer may knock $10,000 off the asking price if your kitchen looks dated.

The fastest, most inexpensive kitchen updates include painting or staining the cabinets and new cabinet hardware, a new backsplash can also be a huge impact on the overall appearance of the kitchen. A real estate professional can help guide your decision with this and keep in mind most real estate agents also have contacts with all sorts of contractors. While I do not recommend new cabinets for your kitchen or baths, if you feel you really need cabinets check out https://www.rtacabinetstore.com. Also for the bathroom Lowes and Home Depot sell vanities with counter and sink, some also include new mirror and they are not expensive.

http://123soldnow.com

Some things to consider: Remove and pack any pots, pans, dishes and bowls that you don't absolutely need during the selling process. Your primary objective is to leave your perspective buyer with the feeling that their kitchen supplies will fit comfortably into your kitchen.

You can also upgrade the faucet, update hardware, and depending on your budget consider new appliances. With a few good looking "shinny" upgrades you can make your buyers feel like they are in a champagne home that you spruced up on a Beer budget. Use neutral-color paint so you can present buyers with a blank canvas where they can start envisioning their own style. If you have a little money to spend, buy one fancy stainless steel appliance. Why one? Because when people see one high-end appliance they think all the rest are expensive too and it updates the kitchen.

Bathrooms

Bathrooms can become a point of contention for buyers if they're not in tip-top shape. Rather than taking on an expensive renovation, make minor upgrades that have an impact such as caulk the tub, re-grout tile, and install new fixtures. Paint or stain the cabinet, replace counter tops. Larger, less costly fixes are also a possibility if you know where to look – a new vanity, for instance, can cost less than $1,000 if you shop around.

Do you still have that old hairdryer under the sink that doesn't work? Have the kids outgrown the bath toys that are cluttering the sides of the bathtub? Like any other part of your home, the bathroom starts feeling small because there is too much stuff.

http://123soldnow.com

Your potential buyers are going to open the cabinets and drawers in your bathroom, really they will. Take a trashcan and thoroughly go through your medicine cabinets, drawers, vanity cabinet and other bathroom storage areas and remove outdated, broken, and underused items. For emergency or once-in-awhile type items – such as first-aid supplies – create a small basket for just these items and throw away old and outdated supplies.

Use only perfect personal accents in the bathroom. It is important that anything left out for visitors to see is pristine. If you have a gorgeous fluffy white bathrobe, hanging it on a decorative hook on the door can be an attractive accent -- but if your robe is more of the nubby blue floral variety, you might want to hide it away. Look at every detail with a visitor's eye -- bars of soap should be fresh and clean, towels spotless, the garbage always emptied.

If you have a glass shower, please take time to remove water spots. Vinegar is an excellent glass cleaner and removes water spots. Make sure the lighting in the bathroom is bright. Check the toilet seat, if you need a new one it is a quick easy fix don't forget to update with a new shower curtain and shower mat.

Take the home out of your house

As previously mentioned, it is important to de-personalize and de-clutter your home. The more personal stuff in your house, the less potential buyers can imagine themselves living there.

What is clutter? Clutter is too much stuff in too small a space; anything that you no longer use or love; anything that leads to a feeling of disorganization. With that as your guiding filter, you can move from room to room, removing everything that resembles clutter.

Are your closets full? Drawers stuffed? Cabinets crammed? Piles spilling over? Do you just have way too much stuff? Do you have too much furniture? Start packing! Remember you are moving so donate, sell or store things you don't need right now so your house can feel spacious and clean to potential buyers.

Need a place to start?

> Junk drawers full of unneeded items (rubber bands, old batteries, or old keys).
> Closets full of clothes you no longer wear.
> Decorations that are no longer meaningful and/or are outdated.

The key is to make each **room** in your **house** feel larger by removing anything that is not needed.

You will want to toss what you don't need. Remember this well-known rule among organization experts: if you haven't used it in a year (some say two), put it in storage, donate, sell or be rid of it!

Tackle each room separately, identify the purpose of each room and then identify the clutter. For example, the bedroom should be a place of intimacy and rest. If there are too many major functions in the room or too many things going on in the space, it will be difficult for a potential buyer to see the real purpose of the room.

Taking the extra minute to put things in their assigned places will help keep clutter at bay. It will save you the stress of being unable to find items. It will also keep your house organized and inviting, and it will ultimately prove to be a huge time saver and give potential buyers a sense of space while they are in your home.

Avoid feeling overwhelmed and remember you have options. Your junk may be someone else's treasure. Have a garage sale. Give to others. This includes family, friends, and charities. Some charities will even pick up the items from your home, saving you extra time and trouble.

After cleaning and working hard, the fun part can begin: organizing those things you actually need and use and want to take with you to your next home. You will most likely find that many seasonal items such as decorations or sports equipment can all be put into a storage unit rather than cluttering your home with them.

We often have too much stuff in one space, making it difficult to use what we do have. In this case, it is important to clean out these spaces, determine the extent to which items are used, and prioritize what is truly useful, pack up what you want to move, sell and give away the rest.

Remove "invisible clutter," the clutter that is often hidden in those rarely visited spaces such as the attic or the garage. After determining the use of every room, try to keep in mind that the garage is the car's room. The U.S. Department of Energy cites that 25 percent of homeowners with two-car garages have too much clutter to store vehicles, and 32 percent only have room for one vehicle. Can you park in your garage? You know the potential buyer wants to see a neat and clean space to park their cars.

De-cluttering your home so that it feels open and spacious, while creating a good sense of flow, will generate a positive response from buyers. Ultimately this will lead to selling your home for more money! Bring back a few elements that will really make your home appealing. Think vases of cut flowers, a basket of fresh farmer's market produce on the kitchen counter or a bowl of lemons beside the sink. Your goal is a clean, not personal, spacious and welcoming house.

Chapter 3

Staging the home for sale

Staging the Living room

Staging your living room is key to a speedy sale because it detracts buyers from perceived flaws of the home. Living room design is much less complex than that of a kitchen or bathroom, so you don't have to spend big on staging to see big results.

One inexpensive way to stage is to switch up the color scheme of the room. To better suit buyer preferences, use neutral-toned items you already own to create a cohesive palette throughout the room—décor magazines employ this visual effect to please reader eyes. Shelve books with similarly-colored spines in a bookcase, place decorative pillows in coordinating, not matching, shades on sofas, side chairs, and tuck children's toys into ornamental boxes that reflect the overall color theme. Remember when selling that less is more! I studied Design in College and my instructor always said, less is more and this is so true when selling your home. It's a quote from Mies van der Rohe, who was an architect, his design style was minimalism. Remember….. Less is more.

You can add a touch of sparkle and a hint of luxury by placing smaller glass accents sparingly throughout the space, on coffee or end tables, bookcases

http://123soldnow.com

or mantels. These touches will draw the eye and add some elegance to the house which will boost perceived value on the part of the buyer and that is a good thing.

Another cost-effective way to stage the living room is to update the window treatments. Steer clear of high-end materials, which are not only expensive, but also may not suit your buyers tastes once you move into your new home. One budget-friendly trick is to hang shower curtains in place of standard drapery, which are durable and come in an array of patterns and colors. Ones with large, pre-cut holes in upscale finishes (think wood) can be threaded through your existing curtain rods, saving you even more money and giving your living room a fresh new look.

The furniture collection in a room should form a restful, symmetrical layout. It's all about balance. There should be between three and ten feet between each seat. Additionally, instead of pushing each piece up against the wall to create more space, give your furniture a bit of breathing room a few inches from the wall. This will make the room appear open and airy.

Staging the Bedrooms

The Master bedroom will be your homebuyers retreat. Ensure all closets, drawers and table surfaces have minimal content. If you need to put belongings in storage, under bed containers, or in others closets, do so!

If you do not have a headboard, please do yourself a favor and get one. You will want to show your bedrooms as a bedroom, do so by removing the home office or exercise equipment from the master bedroom.

http://123soldnow.com

Similarly, often when we have an extra bedroom it becomes additional storage. Remove the items and stage the room accordingly.

Other easy tips include adding a fresh up to date comforter, window coverings, steam clean carpets or replace them and again, paint! If you need to freshen up the paint consider a color in the comforter as an accent wall color.

Create a gender-neutral master bedroom that will appeal to everyone. You can't go wrong with clean, crisp linens, tasteful artwork and a blanket folded at the foot of the bed. **Small changes can have a huge impact.**

If you have a three-bedroom house with a den, the only reason the den can't be considered a bedroom may be because it doesn't have a closet, if you add a closet to that room, you've now got a four-bedroom house. That adds a lot of perceived value to the buyer and you will sell your house for more money.

Staging your Dining Room

When showing your dining room, take care to set the table and make it look inviting and festive by adding a centerpiece or candles. Setting the table really does make a big difference.

Consider a fresh coat of paint, while a dark color on the walls can be effective in cozying up a small space, layers of white and neutral textures can make a small space feel larger. Painting the trim and the walls in similar tones will reduce visual barriers and can effectively enlarge the appearance of your room.

Before *After*

Mirrors can expand the boundaries of your room. Use them to reflect light and space around the room and to double the impact of windows. However, be careful with what the mirrors reflect. If they reflect clutter or the wrong view, they can make a room feel more crowded. Look in the mirror from all angles to determine if it is reflecting a view you like.

Additionally, if you have windows that are lower than your ceiling height, consider hanging curtains and blinds closer to the ceiling. This trick will increase the apparent size of the windows as well as create the illusion of taller ceilings and an overall bigger room.

Dark corners can make a room feel small and depressing. While overhead lighting can be helpful, wall, floor and table lamps will spread light all around the room. This will make the space feel larger and more inviting. This is what buyers want.

http://123soldnow.com

Staging closets

Yes, really! Storage is something every buyer is looking for and can never have enough of. The more clutter you have in your cabinets and closets, the smaller they will feel to a buyer. It makes a big difference to see a closet jam-packed full of clothing compared to one that appears to have plenty of room.

Big secret here, take half the stuff and out of your closets and then neatly organize what's left in there. Buyers will snoop, so be sure to keep all your  closets and cabinets clean and tidy and don't forget the medicine cabinet.

Stage the outdoors

Even if you're current home is a condo with a postage stamp–size balcony you can play it up with a cafe table and chairs, a cheerful tablecloth, and even a little tray of dishes or a vase of flowers. When people look at this scene they won't be thinking "small," they will be thinking, "What a charming spot to have breakfast!"

Basic backyards outfitted with plastic furniture and folding lawn chairs are a thing of the past. Today's outdoor spaces have evolved to become true extensions of the home offering all the style, comfort and function of an interior living area. From furniture and accessories to fully-appointed outdoor kitchens, the lines between indoors and out have blurred beyond distinction, especially in Phoenix because of the nice weather we have all year round.

What to do: With these tips in mind, do a walk-through of your own home, pretending that you're seeing it for the first time. What things have you always meant to fix? What can be taken to storage? Spend a few weekends dealing with all of those nagging projects to get your home in show-worthy condition so you can sell your home for more money.

Chapter 4

The HOME Inspection, it's going to happen, so get ready.

The vast majority of buyers make a purchase offer that's contingent upon receiving a satisfactory report from a certified home inspector. Most home lenders require it and in some cases, may require additional inspections-- such as a termite report- -depending on the state you live in.

If you know a home inspector is going to find something wrong with your house go ahead and fix it first, this will save you time and money later on. One property I sold had a light switch for the pool that was not working, my buyer was not going to purchase the home if the light in the pool did not work, obviously there were other problems and the seller did not want to repair anything, we were days from our scheduled closing buyer and seller simply could not agree, finally the seller gave in and repaired the light switch for the pool light and the buyer went ahead with the purchase. Little things are a big deal to a new home owner. Just imagine, they scrape every penny together to purchase your home, the last thing a buyer wants is a home that needs repairs as soon as they take possession and move in.

It makes more sense to do the small repairs ahead of time rather than wait for a buyer to request it. Buyers may end up asking you to spend $300 on what should cost $100 just to make sure it's done right. Think about the pool light switch, not a big deal but when you are days from your house closing escrow and you need an electrician NOW, you will be forced to hire anyone who will come now, instead of taking care of it in the first place. If you have never looked at a home inspection, they are very detailed and can make the perfect home look like it needs work. So go ahead repair any leaky faucets, leaks under the sink, make sure the air and heat are working properly, repair any windows that do not open, paint the fascia board and the eves of your home, make sure the roof is in good condition and remember that light switch! If you're looking for an idea of what a certain repair will cost you can get a ball park figure by going to http://www.improvenet.com

If you are looking at a major repair, like the roof, or you have an outdated electrical system, you will want to consult with your real estate agent to determine the pros and cons of expense to income from the sale of the home. Investing in maintenance and repairs is not only moneywise but could also be crucial to the sale of your home. Brokers and agents from across the country say the houses that get attention are the ones that are in tip-top shape. I can tell you from my experience buyers love shiny houses.

Start with a couple of hundred dollars on a few minor things. This will increase the value of your house by a few thousand dollars. People are surprised by this because usually they think they have to put in a lot of money to see a big difference in sales price and it really isn't necessary. If you are not sure of the condition of your home, let's say it has been a rental or you have put off a lot of maintenance for years, you can order a home inspection before putting your home on the market. Home inspections cost about $450.00. Then when your buyer orders an inspection you should be in good shape. You can also consult with your real estate agent as we have been through many of them, and can tell you a lot just by looking at your homes over all condition.

So how much should you spend to upgrade your home before selling it?

Remember that the return on investment, or ROI, on home improvements is generally less than 100 percent. For example, say your home is worth approximately $200,000 and you spend $30,000 to remodel the kitchen.

Many people mistakenly believe that the home is now worth $230,000. Then while a remodel certainly adds some value, it's like buying a new car that depreciates in value the moment you drive it off the dealer's lot. I recommend making small upgrades, like replacing the kitchen sink and or faucets throughout the house. Consider updating the counters and or backsplash. Also consider painting or staining your cabinets, updating the hardware and or replacing an old water heater that is full of rust and shows signs of leaking.

If you have a seriously outdated kitchen or bathroom you will generally come out ahead by discounting the asking price instead of a full on remodel so the buyer can choose their own finishes and make it their new home. It's best to keep in mind with this scenario that unless you're willing to discount a home's price well below market value, prospective homebuyers generally won't want to buy a house that needs a lot of work. Investors don't mind, so you may want to consider the option of selling to an investor at a wholesale price. We will cover this option later on in this book.

A home inspection can make or break the sale of your home, get ready and be prepared, when was the last time you crawled into the attic or under the house? Home inspections look into everything, they measure the water pressure coming out of the faucets, the temperature coming out of the heating and cooling vents, they check all of your appliances, the structure of the home, sprinklers in the yard, pool and equipment, trusses in the attic, the roof, and the list goes on. Home inspectors are able to find problems you never knew you had, so get ready because it is going to happen.

Chapter 5

Showing your home to prospective buyers

Now that your home is looking good inside and out, let's talk about showing your home to perspective buyers.

Photography

After you have improved curb appeal, made necessary upgrades, depersonalized and decluttered the interior spaces, consider hiring a professional photographer to take high-quality images in the best light to showcase what your home has to offer.

Most people start their home search online, making photos a crucial part of getting their attention. Homes with professional photos sell faster and for more money than listings that had poorly composed photos. The photos of your home should capture full rooms that are well lit and don't show cluttered or messy spaces because home buyers want to see what your home has to offer and be able to visualize themselves living there. Some agents, such as myself, offer to have professional photos done at no cost to the seller.

See http://123soldnow.com/whatsmyhomeworth

Wash your windows

You have to market your home in such a way as to appeal to the potential buyer's senses and emotions. You want them to feel that your home is the right home for them and their family. Cleaning windows inside and out can be taxing but it makes a noticeable difference. For the exterior sides of the windows, scrub off any accumulated film from tree pollen and polish until glistening. You may want to consider hiring a cleaning service to clean them for you. Buyers will be pleased to see not only a sparkling home outside, but a light-filled interior as well; clean windows really do make a big difference in the buyer's perception of the home, and they won't even know why.

Conceal the critters

You might think a cuddly dog would warm the hearts of potential buyers but you'd be wrong. Not everybody is an animal lover. Buyers don't want to walk in your home and see a bowl full of dog food, smell  the kitty litter box or get pet hair stuck to their clothes. Even worse, you won't want your pet jumping on perspective buyers or barking at them while they are looking at your home. Nothing is more distracting or turns off buyers faster. I have been on showings with clients, where sellers have left pets in the house. We walk in and the only thing we hear is barking and

http://123soldnow.com

lots of it. The buyers cannot look at the home or appreciate all of your hard work because the dogs are barking and distracting the buyers. It is a very good way to make sure the buyers leave the house and never come back. Additionally, a prospective buyer could have a pet allergy and depending on severity, could not even step foot inside your house. Typically, pets in the home can give buyers the impression that your house is not clean especially if they do not like pets. If you're planning an open house, send the critters to a pet hotel for the day and beware of pet odors. If you have pets, get all of your rugs steam cleaned and be extra vigilant about vacuuming and washing surfaces. Take care to hide all pet toys and cat boxes.

Also remove their paraphernalia, such as dog dishes and cat litter boxes (or at least hide them). A prospective buyer shouldn't even know that a pet lives in the home if you can help it.

Light it up

After location, good light is the one thing that every buyer cites that they want in a home When potential buyers enter a room filled with natural light, the more likely they are to envision how they'll incorporate their own color schemes throughout their new potential home. Beautiful sunlight is right outside the window; use it to your advantage by opening all curtains and shades. Use your window treatments strategically to control lighting and to add a decorative touch to windows in the evening hours. The goal, when working with the lighting, is to make your house bright and cheery as this will make your home more sellable. High wattage bulbs tend to make small spaces feel larger while soft lighting brings warmth to empty spaces.

Appeal to the Senses

Most homebuyers know the feeling – the feeling of walking into a house and *knowing* it's the right one for you. While home staging and other tricks may be helping potential buyers *feel* an emotional connection to a home, what many potential sellers don't know is that appealing to all five of the buyer's senses is an important element of the home selling process.

The first thing that triggers a potential buyers "feel" is the way a home smells. Smells are directly linked to our emotions. The cells for our nose carry the signals of smell to our brain's limbic system, and directly to the part of our brain that is involved in emotional learning and memory. This means, if there are any smells that you have a positive association with, you will like the home more. Your home should smell freshly cleaned but not overly fake or have a chemical like odor. If your home feels stuffy, concentrate on circulating fresh air and replace air filters beforehand. Some popular choices for scents within the home are lemon, lavender, or orange. One option is a diffuser with essential oils. To add a personal

touch, consider baking fresh cookies or brewing a fresh pot of coffee before you open your home to the general public, it really makes a difference.

Your taste buds go hand-in-hand with the sense of smell, so why not offer potential buyers coffee or cookies you just prepared? The more domesticated your home feels the more likely potential buyers are to envision themselves transforming your old home into their new home.

Often, light or soft music, think elevator music, can be played during the showing or open house to help create a welcoming atmosphere.

The old adage "you can look, but you can't touch" does NOT apply to potential home buyers. Homebuyers like to touch things and will be all over the door knobs, banisters, and cabinets. You will want to make sure those are clean and free of dust. Use this information to appeal to the buyer's senses and you will evoke emotion which will cause your house to sell quickly and for more money.

Always be ready to show

The more flexible you are about visits, the more people will be able to see your home. Be ready for prospective visitors early in the morning, at night and on weekends, with little notice. Your house needs to be "show-ready" at all times because you never know when your buyer is going to walk through the door. Take measures to ensure that you don't leave dishes in the sink, keep the dishwasher cleaned out, the bathrooms sparkling and make sure there are no dust bunnies in the corners. It's a little inconvenient but it will get your house sold for more money fast.

Although you may want to stick around during a showing, it may not be the best idea. There is definitely an emotional aspect when selling your home, so hovering while a potential buyer is touring your home may make it difficult for them to envision the home as theirs and may feel uncomfortable or feel that they're intruding on your space. Take a breather and go run some errands while your real estate agent does the work.

Chapter 6

Pricing it right

Things to consider when setting your price:

> - How urgently do you need to sell your house?
> - Is a career or job change prompting your relocation?
> - Is your move tied to the school year?
> - Do you have medical concerns?
> - Are you selling due to financial pressures?
> - Do you need to sell because of divorce?
> - Are you behind in payments?
> - Do you owe more than its worth?

I can help you with any of these situations as I have seen them all many times. Typically urgency determines price in the sense that the more quickly you need to sell the lower you'll need to price your house. If you can wait for the ideal offer, you can price your house accordingly or sell for quick cash to an investor.

The best place to start this process is by getting a CMA, which can be obtained through a realtor or go online to http://123soldnow.com/whatsmyhomeworth.

Many times, sellers try to sell property without hiring a real estate professional, because they believe it will save money in the long run. However, I can tell you from experience that a good realtor will save you both money *and* time. Since a real estate agent is paid a percentage of your selling price, it is in their best interest to price it perfectly. Real estate agents want to earn the highest commission possible, but they also want to earn a commission within a reasonable amount of selling time.

The majority of buyers start their home search online. To sell a home, you want to work with a Realtor who will make sure that professional photos, a vibrant description are widely available on multiple websites. More buyers are using mobile phones and tablets to search for homes, so marketing materials should be easy to navigate from those devices, too. This is usually part of an agent's service, but it doesn't hurt to double-check that your listing is on Zillow, Trulia and Realtor.com. It also helps if your agent showcases the home on social media and schedules it on a home tour. We sell as many homes off of Facebook as we do the multiple listing service (MLS).

Choosing the right listing price is one of the most important tips for selling your home quickly. If your home is priced too low, you'll obviously leave money on the table and if it's too high, you will get few offers and watch it get stale on the market. Your price should be competitive. The first week that a listing goes on the market is when it receives nearly four times more visits online than it does a month later. Even if you drop the price later, it won't get the same attention so it's very important to set a good price the first time.

http://123soldnow.com

One tactic to sell your home quickly is to start with a lower asking price,

 usually fifteen to twenty percent off the home's worth. Often a lower starting price will create a bidding war, which is a very good thing if you're the one selling the home. Even in the worst markets, often interested buyers will bid up the price over what it is worth. It takes courage; most sellers just don't want to risk it because there is always the possibility that that you could settle for less then what they wanted, but it's the single best strategy to sell a home in today's market.

Conversely, if you overprice the home, it may sit on the market for months and you will lose a lot more. Sellers often think they should start with a high asking price and then lower it later if the house fails to sell. This can result in a slower sale. The first thirty days your house is listed is the time when your house will see the most activity. During this time, if the price is too high many buyers and their agents will stay away from your house because they assume you are not serious about selling or you are unwilling to negotiate.

Overpriced homes that stay on the market for 90 to 120 days become extremely difficult to sell. After a home sits on the market for an extended period of time, many people will *assume* that it hasn't sold because something is wrong with it. When I am out with clients looking at homes one of the first questions I am asked besides price is how many days has it been on the market. If the listing is within the first week my buyers get excited about the home. They think they may have found a really good one before anyone else. If the listing is over 30 days on the market they are disappointed, thinking it can't possibly be a good home. It is very important to set the price according to your competition and see the other homes in your area that are for sale. Every agent knows the old adage, "Homes that don't show well don't close well."

Generally home sellers think the house is worth more than the suggested listing price and home buyers have a much better grasp on what the home is worth because they are looking at many homes in the same general area. Sellers need to set a price to get the buyers attention and buyers need to feel they are getting a good deal. Remember the market sets the price. Good Real estate professionals know the local market and will review comparable sales to make sure you set a realistic price.

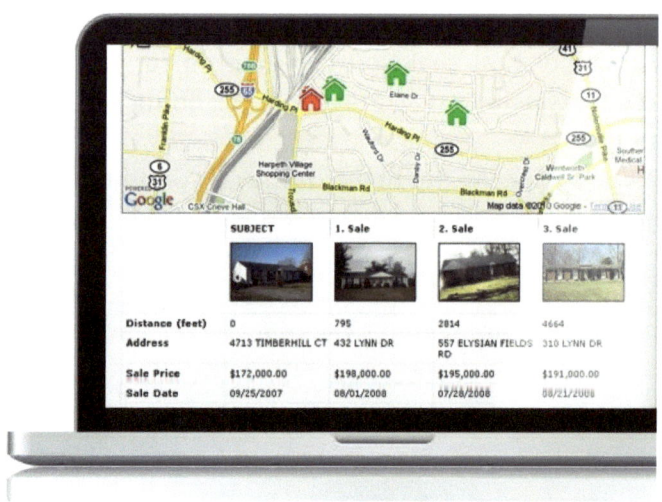

Chapter 7

Let's talk about selling to investors.

You have decided to sell your home. We went over the first option for a traditional sale with tips and tricks for getting the right agent, making small

repairs and went over things like decluttering, staging and showing. Because selling a home can be an emotionally and physically exhausting process, some people don't want to go through their home as suggested by the first part of this book. Now we will now take a look at the second  option, selling to investors. This option requires very little time and effort on your part. In my experience, this is the one proven method to get your house sold in any market without any hassle or extreme cost.

This strategy is mainly for people who are willing to sacrifice a bit on the sales price in exchange for a fast convenient sale, without issues. If you need to sell quickly, such as days or weeks rather than months, investors can close on your home quickly. This method is also convenient if you do not want to make repairs or worry about cleaning up the house before listing it.

Real estate investors typically pay with cash ensuring a quick close and the funds in your hands quickly as well. The only potential cost or draw back to working with an investor is that an investor can't pay full retail value for a house. Think of it like a car, most people trade in their car to eliminate hassle and headache of trying to sell it themselves, making two payments at the same time or looking for a new car without a car. We all know the dealership is paying a discounted rate and will turn around and sell your car for a markup and make a profit. However because of the convenience and

http://123soldnow.com

speed, it makes sense for you to sell it for less money in return for not having to worry about taking it home, making more payments or spending money on marketing it. The dealer saves you time and money, much like an investor will on your house.

What is a real estate investor?

A real estate investor is someone who invests in real estate. Think of those "We Buy Houses" signs, that's most likely a real estate investor looking for home sellers to purchase properties from. An investor will evaluate the house, come up with a value for it, determine if any repairs are needed, find out what your goals are, and make an offer that fits the investors buying criteria and helps you reach your goals. As the seller, you then have the option to look at the offer and decide if it works for you.

Joint ventures, such as wholesaling and property management, are ways investors can profit from real estate. Investors look to buy houses at discounts that allow them to turn a small profit on the deal. This means you will be selling at a lower price, but for some people it makes sense because by selling to an investor you eliminate commissions, home repairs, staging and get a much faster timeline to sell your house. For those on a very tight timeline, real estate investors are usually more than willing to buy homes within a few days, effectively saving owners from foreclosure, bankruptcy and many other situations that would require selling right away.

Sell quickly for less

If you are struggling financially, selling to an investor means you won't need to spend money that you really don't have making repairs on a home you are leaving. Investors buy "as is" because they already plan to renovate and repair the property to resell it or rent it to someone else for a profit.

Investors use cash to pay for homes or private lenders to make quick, cash like purchases and the fees on these loans are usually around 12-16 percent annual interest and 4 to 6 up front points. This can easily put an investor's holding costs at around 10-12 percent on just a six month deal.

Most real estate investors are already down 25 percent before they even start to think about renovation costs and some sort of profit. This may seem high but it just means the average gross margin for a real estate investor is about 40 to 50 percent and that is in line with other industries, so they need to buy your home for less than market value.

When you decide to sell, you may not be able to accept offers from people who need a loan to buy your home. If a home is in serious disrepair banks will not give buyers a loan. Part of the importance of an appraisal early on is that it tells a lender the condition of a property. If a home has roof issues, foundation issues or even exposed wires, you may be stuck until someone else pays for the repairs. Whatever amount your neighbor got isn't necessarily what you will get. Don't be angry with a lower offer from an investor if it allows you to benefit from the sale; it's better than losing out on your equity altogether.

If you're interested in connecting with an investor to purchase your home simply fill out our online form with the address of the property you're selling and your contact info, once we get the address we can start pulling up some basic information about the property and the area. We will then give you a call to discuss your particular situation and needs and match you with an investor to make you an offer. Simply go to http://123soldnow.com/sellitnow

Keep foreclosure off your credit rating

Homeowners all over the country are facing foreclosure and let's face it, predatory lending, and job loss can take its toll. When you first fall into default and discover that you may never catch up on all of the payments and late fees, a notice of foreclosure is no big surprise. You're probably wondering, "How do I sell my house fast?"

With the threat of foreclosure looming, a real estate agent can help get you more time in your home and help you find a new place to live in addition to finding and investor to pay cash for your home before the auction date plus saving your credit from having a foreclosure on it. Some people can resort to taking out a loan or having a family member or friend pay for extensive repairs. By selling to an investor this isn't what needs to happen. To be clear, foreclosure is always an option, but when it seems like you have run out of options, contact a real estate agent who can help with selling to an investor before the auction date or pursuing a short sale which will give you more time. Typically either is a better course of action than letting your house go back to the bank. This allows you to save your credit to some extent. In the event you are in foreclosure do not move out of the house, contact a real estate agent for help. Foreclosures can take up to two years and this leaves you with a lot of time to find other solutions to your money situation. Even if you are already in foreclosure **don't panic,** you still have lots of options and time, contact a real estate agent, they can help. The house is still yours to sell up to the date of the trustee's sale. Staying in the

house allows you stay in control of the moving date and really is less painful than the bank taking your house from you.

If you are in foreclosure and have moved out of your house, it is still your house. You can still sell the house right up to the date of the trustee's sale. Please contact a licensed real estate professional as soon as possible prior to the trustee's sale date *there are always options and help is always available to you* not to mention limiting the damage to your credit. If you are in foreclosure **don't panic** help is available.

A foreclosure keeps you from getting a loan to purchase a new home because it stays on your credit report for seven years, a short sale stays with you for two years and bankruptcy stays with you for four years. When the time comes for you to purchase a new home, I work with lenders that can help you repair your credit and in some cases help you get a new FHA loan within three years. Sometimes life just happens and you become a motivated seller. This could be due to divorce, a death in the family, loss of a job. Perhaps you have inherited a home and are out of state or maybe you are a landlord and are just tired of rentals and repairing toilets.

I do believe your house is your biggest asset. I would not recommend selling quickly for cash to an investor unless you have become a motivated seller, in which case I do recommend selling to an investor above letting your home go back to the bank.

How an investor works

A short sale is tailor-made for selling to an investor because short sales are "as is" sales. That means the bank isn't going to pay for any repairs. You, as the seller, aren't required to make any repairs either.

The major difference when doing a short sale with an investor is that your agent still needs to provide the bank with the highest and best offer. Note, the highest and best offer will be considered, not just the highest. An investor can move quickly to correct the situation because they pay for the property in cash. With a short sale your real estate agent will take over communicating with your lender to ensure that the process goes quickly, smoothly and without a hitch.

Investors add value to distressed properties. For example, if all of the homes in your neighborhood are selling in the $500,000 range and a short sale closes for $475,000, it adversely affects the value of all of your neighbor's homes. If I can buy that home, rehabilitate it and sell it for $525,000, I help strengthen values in your neighborhood. However, no matter how similar properties look, you must remember that every property is unique. If your property has more problems than solutions or if repairs to your home will eat up all of your spare time and money then a quick sale might make sense for you.

Real estate investors are skilled at bringing a distressed property back to its former glory. Because they deal with all types of property problems every day, they won't require any extensive repairs, cleanup or ask for other contingencies to be met in order to buy your house quickly. Another added benefit is that you won't have to suffer the inconvenience of having strangers traipsing through your home, criticizing its current condition.

If an investor asks you for money up front then this is a scam. No investor will take money from you. In fact they will either give you a small amount of money to make the contract legal or you will collect an EMD (earnest money deposit) which will be held at a title company either of your choosing or an agreed upon Title Company for you and the investor to solidify the deal.

How to Sell Your Home Quickly

The best way to sell your home quickly is to find a real estate investor who is ready to make a fast purchase. The investor will come to your home and assess what they can do to help you in your situation. You don't need the investor to fall in love with your house because decisions to purchase — or not purchase — a home is strictly economic. The investor will look at all the aspects of your situation and get an offer to you on your property. You will quickly have an option on the table to solve the problem of selling your house quickly.

Real estate investors are sometimes willing to team up with homeowners to help them keep their homes — either permanently or temporarily. Although these investors normally purchase properties with the expectation that the previous owners vacate the premises, this isn't always the case. You can usually find reputable investors through trustworthy real estate agents, attorneys (especially foreclosure and bankruptcy attorneys), and perhaps even local banks. An investor can wholesale your home or repair it and sell it on the MLS and they're looking for deals all the time.

http://123soldnow.com

If the offer works for you, then the investor will help guide you through the process which is pretty simple. Here's what will happen:

- ➢ A Purchase and Sales agreement will be signed by both parties
- ➢ You will get the chance to have your attorney review the agreement
- ➢ You open escrow with a title company who oversees the closing
- ➢ A mutually-agreeable closing date will be set — often within days, instead of   the months that traditional real estate transactions usually take
- ➢ You avoid having to pay real estate commissions

To access our data base of investors who are looking for properties and ready to make a purchase go to http://123soldnow.com/sellitnow

I use an easy 1-2-3 approach

- ➢ Step 1 — take two minutes to contact us today http://123soldnow.com/sellitnow
- ➢ Step 2 — come to an agreement that works for both you and your potential buyer
- ➢ Step 3 — you collect your money when closing escrow

http://123soldnow.com

My investors buy all types of property: residential, multi-family, commercial, lots, land and more. I handle all sorts of problem tenants, eliminating nightmare calls and any problems that come with being a landlord. I can eliminate the home owner's stress of liability, vandalism, and theft on vacant properties. I can give you a no obligation offer within days and sometimes within hours. This takes care of the waiting and wondering that occurs when selling your home on the market in the traditional way. I can customize the transaction to fit your needs, making the process as easy and comfortable as possible for you.

Carefully Consider Offers, and Be Prepared to Negotiate

We are in the home stretch now.

You have an offer on your home; an experienced listing agent will know a good offer when they see it. A great agent can guide you through the whole process and advise you when to negotiate prices and terms. A quality agent will know

what's "normal" when it comes to offers, and when someone is trying to get a bargain. You should consider all the terms of the offer, not just the price, to make sure you get the best deal for your situation.

Visit 123soldnow.com for more information on selling your home with an experienced real estate agent, or to request a free, no-obligation consultation on your home's value.

visit http://123soldnow/whatsmyhomeworth to get a free CMA for your property.

http://123soldnow.com

Some common questions

What if I need Money to move? No problem, we can close on your house so you can get your money and even give you 30 days to move from the property after closing. I even have an assisted moving program where they actually do your move for you.

How long does it take to close on my property? We can close within 2 weeks or less as long as there is clear title. First we sign a contract at the agreed price to start the process and I will take it from there. I will handle all the details to get to the closing so you can get the cash you need.

What if I'm behind on my payments or in foreclosure? It's not too late; you still have time to sell your home, up to the day before it is set for auction but time is of the essence. Contact me now before it is too late. I will match your property with one of our investors. You still have options and I have answers. Let me help you out of an ugly situation.

What if I owe back taxes? No Problem! The delinquent taxes will come out of the proceeds at closing. You do not have to pay or have any out of pocket fees prior to closing.

What if I still owe on my mortgage? As long as the numbers work it's no problem. The title company will verify the payoff from the mortgage company and the payoff amount will come out of your proceeds at closing.

What if I inherited a property and need to sell it? Give me a call. We will handle all the paperwork to make a smooth closing. I can even secure the property for you and handle all the estate paperwork required to get to closing.

What if I have outstanding liens and judgments' against my property? The title company will do a title search and if there are any liens or judgments against the property they will examine it further and verify it, if it does in fact belong to you or the property they will take the amount out of your proceeds.

http://123soldnow.com

What if I'm upside down on my mortgage? In a slow real estate market, selling your house can be difficult– especially if you owe more on your mortgage than your house is worth. Contact us and we can discuss the specifics of your situation and help you find a win-win solution whether you need more time in your home or cash to move.

What if I already have a real estate agent, can you still buy my house? Yes, just give me a call so we can get the information and get started on an offer from one of our investors now.

Chapter 8

Rentals

We have gone over a traditional sale, and selling to an investor. Another option may be to rent your home instead of selling it. Rentals are definitely one of my favorite subjects. You know how I just love positive cash flow! In some cases renting your home may be an alternative to selling your house.

Let's say your mortgage payment is $1200.00 per month and rents in your area are $1600.00 to $1800.00 per month. There you have your positive cash flow of $400.00 to $600.00 per month. You can reach out to your real estate professional to see what the going rate for rent is in your area. Another way to check is to look on http://craigslist.org.

If you are in a position where you need to move, and will have positive cash flow from your house, I highly recommend this option. Keep in mind, not only are your renters paying off your mortgage for you, they are sending you extra money each month all while your home's value increases over the years. Talk about making your money work for you!

You will encounter issues with tenants, like replacing toilets or calling the handyman because there is a leak under the sink. Sometimes you may need to replace a dishwasher but when you add it all up, not a big cost for a big return. Some people simply cannot deal with having a rental, so you could give your home to a property management firm to take care of the tenants for you.

Most property management firms will charge 10% of the monthly rent; they collect the rent for you, call the plumber when needed, and handle any other situations that may arise. If you choose to rent on your own, you will need a lease with your tenant. You can get one from your real estate professional, and there are leases available for free on the internet you could use as well.

Some landlords do not want to deal with repairs and they pay for a home warranty for the property, then when there is a problem the tenant calls the home warranty firm and pays the service call fee and the repair is made, of course this is written into the lease.

I would say the biggest problem with having a rental is when the tenant moves you need to go in and freshen the house. You will need to paint, and clean or replace the carpet after each tenant. You may like keeping your house and having a rental depending on your circumstances. This is another option I recommend you consider.

There is also another way, turn your home into a vacation rental. Vacation rentals tend to be in better condition over the long hall because guests do not stay for years, they stay for days, weeks or months. Your cleaning crew goes in after each rental, cleans, and lets you know if anything is missing or damaged. Vacation rentals also command more money. Depending on where you live, in most cases, your weekly rental rate for a vacation home will be as much as a monthly tenant would pay you for a whole month.

Vacation rentals do need to be furnished and have cookware in the kitchen; many families prefer vacationing in a home rather than a hotel. Take a look at http://vrbo.com to see what your home could rent for, you may be pleasantly surprised.

One of my clients purchased a home for his children to live in while they attended NAU in Flagstaff. The children all graduated and the oldest child lived in the home for a few years after college, got married and was purchasing his own home. My client wanted to rent this home. Since he told me that he always wanted to have a home in the pines and could never enjoy it, I suggested he turn the home it into a vacation rental. He placed the home for rent on vrbo in October and by the end of December he had collected rental income to cover the mortgage payments for a full year. In fact he was so excited about the vacation rental experience and the income he also placed his own home on vrbo and in six months has received rental income to cover the mortgage payments for both of the homes for an entire year, not to mention he now has the opportunity to stay in his home in Flagstaff when he wants to.

I do the same with the condos at the beach, I go when I can and when I am not there they are making money for me, and pay for themselves. What's not to love?

If you are interested in purchasing your first rental or need help with property management and are in the Phoenix area, feel free to reach out to me.

Chapter 9

I am here to help

I have been buying and selling houses for over 25 years. I have been investing in real estate, selling real estate for sellers and finding homes for buyers during this time. As a result I have a database full of buyers and  investors and can get you a buyer or an investor to buy your house. The investors I work with can buy your house even if your house has zero (or even negative) equity, even if it is in such a poor condition that no bank is willing to finance any potential buyers, even if it has liens, code violations, and other legal problems attached to it. I know professional home buyers and we have the real estate knowledge, legal resources, and funds available to fix most real estate problems.

Referrals generate a sizable portion of a real estate agent or investor's business, so it is critical that agents and investors treat others with respect. This includes business partners, associates, clients, renters and anyone with whom the agent or investor has a business relationship with. Effective real estate agents pay attention to detail, listen and respond to complaints and concerns, and represent their business in a positive and professional manner as well as do what is in the best interest of the real estate agents clients. If you're ready to sell your home and need some input on what needs to be done for a traditional sale, reach out to me, I have contacts for

http://123soldnow.com

handy men, contractors, carpet installers, granite whatever your specific needs are chances are I have been there and done that and I am happy to share and make your selling experience a good one for you.

Weigh your options

I love selling houses, and I am passionate about helping my sellers get ready for a sale. I will help you get through the process with my years of experience with ease. You're ready to sell your house. You now know what you need to do to get it sold. Follow the steps outlined here and you will be on your way to a new home. It is also a lot of fun to buy a house fix it up

and sell it for a profit. If you are a motivated seller I will get you an offer on your home from an investor or list it for you in the MLS whichever is best for your situation. If you choose to take an offer from one of our investors, look it over, pass it by people you trust, and take your time to decide. There's no pressure. If you feel that it helps you reach your goals, great. We can close quickly, no fees, no commissions, and the investor will pay closing costs.

Visit 123soldnow.com

Good luck on the sale of your house! I hope this book has helped you make sense of your options when selling your house or choosing to put it up for rent. I will help you move forward with what makes sense for you and your goals, I am here to help. In some instances working with a reputable real estate agent is the best route... and in some cases selling to an investor is the best route to getting your home sold now, we also covered two ways you can rent your home. Rents are high, and vacation rentals are an awesome alternative for generating income from your property.

This book has given you several options for achieving your goal of selling your home, the first step is really easy and free; begin learning about your local market and the value of your home. You are armed with the information you need to sell your house for more money now. Whatever your reason for selling I know you will make the right decision and I wish you all the best, I want to be a part of your success story, I know houses, please always feel free to reach out to me.

You can get your FREE CMA by going to
http://123soldnow.com/whatsmyhomeworth

www.ingramcontent.com/pod-product-compliance
Lightning Source LLC
Chambersburg PA
CBHW040844180526
45159CB00001B/309